On Edge of Extinction

Claire Craig
Sharon Dalgleish
Ian Rohr

Brainwaves Purple
On the Edge of Extinction
1 86509 831 0 (Paperback)
1 86509 850 7 (Hardback)

All rights reserved. No part of this publication may be reproduced, stored in a retrieval system or transmitted in any form or by any means, electronic, mechanical, photocopying, recording, or otherwise, without the prior written permission of the publisher.

Copyright © 2003 Blake Publishing
Reprinted 2006

Published by Blake Education Pty Ltd
ABN 074 266 023
Locked Bag 2022
Glebe NSW 2037
Ph: (02) 8585 4085
Fax: (02) 8585 4058
Email: mail@blake.com.au
Website: www.blake.com.au

Series publisher: Sharon Dalgleish
Designer: Cliff Watt
Illustrators: Lloyd Foye and Cliff Watt
Photo research: Tracey Gibson

Picture Credits; pg 8-9 (bottom) photolibrary.com; pg 9 (top) AAP Image; pg 11 (top) S. Humphreys/Nature Focus/Australian Museum, (bottom) Nature Focus/Australian Museum; pg 15 APL/Corbis; pg 16 (top) S. Humphreys/Nature Focus/Australian Museum; pg 17 (bottom) APL/Corbis; pg 19 (top) APL/Corbis; pg 25 © 2003 Jon S. Berndt All Rights Reserved; pg 26 (bottom) Mary Evans Picture Library; pg 27 Mary Evans Picture Library; pg 28-29 photolibrary.com.

Printed in Australia by Printing Creations

Contents

- **Dead and Gone** 4
  - Mammoths—What, Where, Why? 6
  - A Tale of Extinction 10

- **Too Close to the Edge** 12
  - Danger—Humans Ahead! 14
  - Nowhere to Live 18

- **Back From the Edge** 22
  - A Siberian Success Story 24
  - Bison on the Brink 26

  - **Fact File** 30
  - **Glossary** 31
  - **Index** 32

Dead and Gone

Simion Jarkov couldn't believe his eyes. There before him, poking out of the icy Siberian ground, were two huge arched tusks.

It was 1997 and Simion, a reindeer herder, had just found the tusks of a woolly mammoth. Tests later showed that the tusks had been frozen for 20 000 years!

Woolly mammoths became extinct, or died out, between 10 000 and 20 000 years ago. But some animals were around until much more recent times. The thylacine was hunted to extinction only last century. The last individual died alone in a zoo in 1936. We know why the thylacine became extinct, but with other **species**, such as the mammoth, we are still searching for answers.

MAMMOTHS—WHAT, WHERE AND WHY?

What were mammoths, where did they live and why aren't any left alive today? Meet the mighty mammoths, and maybe you can figure out why these big beasts are now extinct.

Animals are different shapes and sizes depending on the conditions where they live.

Living on Ice

Mammoths were mammals that lived in Europe, Siberia and North America. Different species lived from five million to just 4 000 years ago. For most of this time, the world was very cold and large rivers of ice called glaciers covered much of the land.

Adult woolly mammoths could stand 3.3 metres tall and weigh 6.3 tonnes. They had long curvy tusks, and looked like elephants in need of a haircut. Underneath their long, shaggy outer coats, they had another coat of short, thick hairs. They had several layers of fat and a shoulder hump with stored reserves for when there was no food around.

Purpose-Built For Snow and Ice

Body hump
This was like a backpack to store fat.

Ears
These were very small. Large ears could get frostbite and fall off!

Outer coat
Hairs up to ?m long covered the body.

Tusks
These were nearly 3 m long in males.

Trunk
Like an elephant's trunk, this was a nose and an upper lip. The mammoth sucked up water through the trunk and squirted it into its mouth.

Feet
It was quite a task to keep a mammoth on its feet! Mammoth feet were flat and had rough skin on the bottom so the mammoth didn't slide on the ice.

Undercoat
Much shorter hairs grew close together next to the body to keep the mammoth really warm.

7

Different Theories

Fossils can give us much information about the lives of mammoths, but scientists still do not know why the mammoth died out. Some believe that the mammoths died out naturally as the climate changed. Woolly mammoths were well suited to living in a cold climate. As the world became warmer, new plants and animals began to **evolve**. Perhaps the grasses and plants that woolly mammoths ate to survive no longer grew in this new, warmer world.

Other scientists think that humans hunted the woolly mammoths until there were none left. Ancient cave paintings show early humans killing mammoths with spears. But one woolly mammoth would have kept a family supplied with food and clothes for a long time. Another theory suggests that new diseases carried by humans and their dogs may have driven the mammoth to the edge of extinction, and then beyond.

A fossil of a mammoth

tusk · rib bone · skull · leg bone

A scientist takes some mammoth hair to examine under a microscope. Any grass or pollen caught in the hair will tell about the plants that grew when mammoths lived.

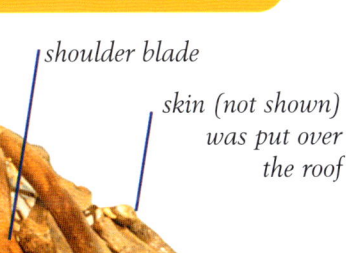

shoulder blade

skin (not shown) was put over the roof

leg bone

 **COULD MAMMOTHS LIVE AGAIN?**

Some people want to clone a woolly mammoth using an elephant as the mother! Most scientists agree that this can't be done. They need the complete **DNA** of an animal before it can be cloned. Cells begin to break down once an animal dies, and the DNA in woolly mammoth cells is too old and damaged to be cloned.

Stone age people used mammoths for food, clothes—and housing. This hut was made between 10 000 and 45 000 years ago out of mammoth bones.

A Tale of Extinction

The Tasmanian tiger, or thylacine, was an unusual and interesting animal. Unfortunately it was also the farmer's enemy and was shot to extinction.

A Shrinking Home

We know that the thylacine once lived in New Guinea and mainland Australia because fossils have been found in these places. But these populations died out—killed by the introduced dingoes, or wild dogs, of the Aboriginal peoples. The rugged island of Tasmania then became the thylacine's last refuge.

Not Just Tasmanian...

Thylacine fossils have been found in New Guinea and mainland Australia. In 1965, a mummified thylacine was found in a cave on the Nullabor Plain. It was over 3 000 years old.

Key
- fossil
- mummy

New Guinea

Australia

Tasmania

10

A Price on Its Head

When European farmers arrived in Tasmania, they believed the thylacines were responsible for killing sheep. In 1888, a **bounty** was put on the thylacine's head. Killing them was now a profitable business encouraged by the government. The thylacine's days were numbered. The last known thylacine died in Hobart Zoo in 1936. It died from the cold because the zoo keeper forgot to lock it in its hut for the night. Today, people sometimes claim to have seen a strange striped animal in the dense Tasmanian bush, but scientists agree that the thylacine is gone forever.

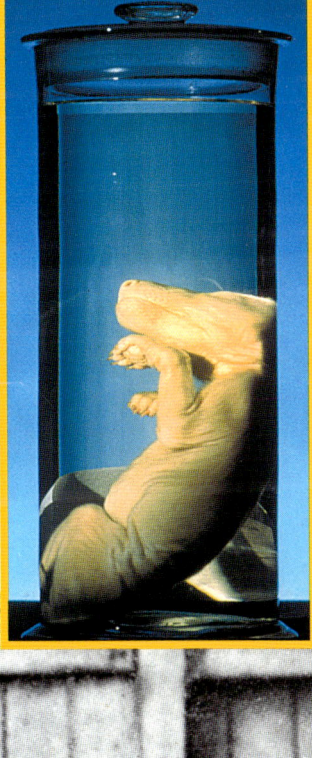

Some scientists hope to clone a thylacine from the remains of a pup that was preserved in alcohol in 1866.

The last thylacine at Tasmania's Hobart Zoo.

11

Too Close to the Edge

The hunter raises his rifle and takes aim. The rhino is in range. A squeeze on the trigger and the rhino falls in a cloud of dust, kicks a few times, then lies still.

People kill animals for many reasons. Sometimes it's for food. Many endangered animals are hunted because their skins, horns, teeth and tails are worth a lot of money. Sometimes animals die because people clear or harm natural **habitats**. And sometimes people kill animals out of fear, or just because they can.

Though charging rhinos or hungry crocodiles can be dangerous to us, we are much more deadly to them. Unfortunately, for too many animals we are the most dangerous of all.

DANGER—HUMANS AHEAD!

Over the last one hundred years about three species per day have become extinct. One of the causes is the over-hunting by humans. Even worse, some scientists estimate that this will rise to 30 species per day over the next one hundred years.

Rhinos in the Spotlight

Rhinos are powerful and fast, but that does not protect them from human hunters and metal bullets. According to the International Rhino Foundation, 96 per cent of the black rhino population died out between 1972 and 1992.

Rhinos are worth more money dead than alive. Their horns are used as ingredients in medicines and potions, as knife handles and cups, and are worth their weight in gold. It is now illegal to hunt or trade in rhino products but prices are so high that **poachers** are willing to break the law. People are working to save the rhino and things have improved. Breeding programs in zoos and protected reserves in the wild are helping, but there is still a long way to go.

If people stopped buying products made from rhino horns, poachers would stop killing the animals.

TOTAL NUMBER OF WILD BLACK RHINOS

The dramatic plunge in black rhino numbers came to a halt in 1996. It shows what people can achieve when they focus their attention to save a species.

KEY 🦏 = 5 000 Rhinos

Year		Count
1970	🦏🦏🦏🦏🦏🦏🦏🦏🦏🦏🦏🦏🦏	65 000
1980	🦏🦏🦏	14 785
1984	🦏🦏	8 800
1994	🦏	2 300
1996	🦏	2 408
1999	🦏	2 704
2001	🦏	3 100

Some conservationists believe that the only way to save black rhinos is to chop off their horns.

These goods were confiscated by airport customs.

Crocodiles on the Run

With their powerful jaws and at least 60 strong teeth, crocodiles tend to get bad press. Most people fear crocodiles, but crocodiles have more to fear from us. Hunted for their skins to make luggage, handbags, wallets and shoes, crocodiles have been over-hunted to the point where many species are in danger of dying out completely.

Cocodile Line-Up

Name	Red List Status*
Siamese Crocodile	CR
Philippine Crocodile	CR
Orinoco Crocodile	CR
Cuban Crocodile	EN
Broad-Snouted Crocodile	VU
American Crocodile	VU

* see page 17

The Cuban crocodile is only found in the wild in the Zapata Swamp region, Cuba.

In some countries there are now farms where crocodiles are bred and killed to make the products that were once made from wild animals. Some **conservationists** are against any killing. Others argue that it is the only way to stop the slaughter of the animals in the wild. They also say that it ensures a breeding stock for the species. Farm-bred crocodiles can be released into the wild in areas where there are few or no crocodiles left.

RED LIST

The World Conservation Union gathers expert information from around the world and compiles it into a Red List of threatened animal species. Each species is given a code showing just how close it is to the edge. Scientists then try to decide if a species can be protected in its natural habitat or if it needs to be conserved in a zoo.

Crocodile farms like this one are helping to maintain crocodile populations.

Red List Codes

Code	Classification	Meaning
EW	Extinct in the Wild	a species known only to survive in captivity
CR	Critically Endangered	species at immediate risk of dying out
EN	Endangered	species that may be extinct in the near future
VU	Vulnerable	species at risk in the longer term
NT	Near Threatened	a species likely to be threatened in the near future
LC	Least Concern	a species that is widespread

NOWHERE TO LIVE

When human activity affects where an animal lives, some species are left with nowhere to go. Habitat loss is an even bigger threat to the natural world than over-hunting.

The only species not affected by habitat loss are those that benefit from human activity, such as rats and cockroaches!

At Home in the Rainforest

Rainforests cover only a small area of the world, but they are very important to life on Earth. More than half of the world's wildlife lives in these forests. As the human population grows, rainforests are being cleared to make land for farming, and for roads and towns.

In Indonesia, huge areas of forest have been cleared so that introduced tree species can be planted. Fires are used to clear native forests, but often they burn out of control, killing native plants and animals.

The woolly spider monkey, or muriqui, lives high in the branches of the trees in the South American rainforests. It roams from tree to tree, looking for fruit, leaves and flowers to eat. In 1500 there would have been about 400 000 swinging in the treetops. Today, there are only between 700 and 1 000 left.

Scientists estimate that 195 **primate** species and **subspecies** are now threatened with extinction. That's one in three! The main cause is habitat loss.

Woolly spider monkey

Orangutans are also endangered. These large apes live high in the treetops of the rainforests of Borneo and Sumatra.

Lost before It's Found

Then there are the animals, insects and plants that we don't know about yet. Only about 10 per cent of living species in the world have actually been identified and many thousands of undiscovered species live in rainforests. As rainforests disappear, some species are dying out faster than scientists can name them. This means that valuable information about all kinds of living things will be lost forever, before it is even found.

> Two and a half square kilometres of rainforest in South America can contain more than 1 000 species of plants.

WILL OUR RAINFORESTS LAST?

Not if we don't change our ways, they won't! Rainforests take millions of years to grow and are being cleared at an alarming rate all over the world. In Africa's Congo Basin they are being destroyed so quickly that there may be none left by 2050. If we humans don't alter our forestry and farming methods, and soon, we will lose these cradles of life forever.

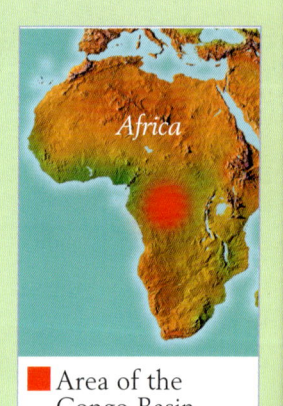

Area of the Congo Basin

In addition to cutting down the rainforests, humans are causing habitat loss in other ways too. The Earth is warming faster than at any time in the past 10 000 years. This enhanced greenhouse effect is being driven by gases produced in huge amounts by our fires, cars and factories. These gases trap heat in the atmosphere. Many scientists estimate that the greenhouse effect is likely to raise world temperatures by 2°C by 2030. Many species will not be able to move to suitable habitats to keep up with the changes.

Sea temperatures in coral reefs only need to rise 1°C above normal for coral to weaken and 'bleach', or lose its colour. In 1998, coral bleaching was reported in 60 countries.

Polar bears hunt on the ice in winter and then sleep through the summer. As the weather gets warmer, the ice is melting earlier. The bears have less time to store up fat for the long summer without food.

Back From the Edge

Time ran out for the mammoth and thylacine. Will we be able to rescue other species before it's too late?

The American bison and the Siberian tiger might not seem to have much in common, but both these magnificent animals have faced extinction. Guns have killed them where they stood, and axes and tractors have cleared their habitats.

There is a growing worldwide awareness that animals, plants and the planet are important. Were it not for the efforts of individuals and organisations, these two big animals might now be only photographs and memories.

A Siberian Success Story

More tigers lurked in the Siberian woods than anyone thought. Finding 600 instead of an expected 300 has increased the chance that the magnificent Siberian tiger will survive.

The Siberian tiger is the largest tiger. A male can be up to 3.5 m long from head to tail.

Good News

Conservationists were thrilled to find out that the Siberian tiger population was twice as big as believed. Siberian tigers live in the dense forests of Siberia. This cold and wild area is called the taiga (TIE-ga) and is vast enough to help the tigers hide from us. Poachers kill some, and forestry and mining have an impact on their habitat. But for now, the tiger seems safe. Unfortunately, if global warming continues, pressure will grow to clear the taiga and make it suitable for farming.

Safe behind Bars

Captive breeding programs are also helping the tigers out. In these programs, animals are moved to a zoo where they can breed. Any offspring can then be released into the wild. There are now over 300 Siberian tigers in zoos around the world. What we now need to do is protect enough of their natural habitat so they too can live the wild life.

Rambo was part of the breeding program at the Houston Zoo, US. He fathered three cubs which have gone to other breeding programs around the world. Sadly, he died in 2001.

WHY IS IT TOUGH AT THE TOP?

At the top of every food chain is a big **predator**. But in a food chain, there are always fewer predators than **prey**. So if something other than the natural cycle of births and deaths reduces predator numbers, they are at risk of extinction. Massive habitat loss and over-hunting have reduced the numbers of most top predators to dangerously low numbers.

BISON ON THE BRINK

Sixty million bison once covered the North American prairie like a great brown blanket. By 1860, fewer than a thousand remained.

Wrong Place, Wrong Time

The bison, also commonly known as buffalo, were descended from animals that had crossed into the Americas 200 000 years ago. Although they were hunted by Native Americans, it was the arrival of new settlers and their guns that spelt disaster for the bison.

Bison are up to 2 m tall at the shoulder and 3.8 m from nose-tip to tail.

The settlers wanted land, but the bison covered it as far as the eye could see. They wanted meat and hides, and the bison could provide both. As the west opened up, and roads and rail lines moved across the prairies, the slaughter became more and more intense.

Hunters would board trains, sit by an open window, and shoot as many bison as they could as the train rolled along. Thousands of corpses were left rotting on the prairie, shot for no reason except that they were big, easy targets and they were in the way.

'Buffalo Bill' Cody bragged that he killed 4 280 head of buffalo in a 17-month shooting spree.

People from the Crow tribe drying bison meat. Native Americans used just about every part of the bison—nothing was wasted. The skins or hides were used to make clothing, ropes, saddles and shoes. And the horns and bones could be made into knives, arrows or shovels.

The Tide Turns
What had been the bison's grazing lands were becoming cleared, fenced and settled. The prairies were shrinking and the Native Americans had been moved to **reservations**. The bison was in big trouble.

Then, about a hundred years ago, there was a change in people's thinking. The government passed laws to protect the few small herds still surviving. Reserves were then set up so those herds would be safe. Some farmers began breeding the animals in captivity.

Now there are over 30 000 bison spread across Canada and the US, in national and state parks, and on private farms. The bison is off the endangered list. The days when the American bison covered the plains are now history. But, due to a change of heart, people who cared, and some practical solutions, our world won't lose the bison.

A 2 000-plus bison herd now roams Yellowstone National Park.

We can stop extinction!

Fact File

The Ten Most Critically Endangered Mammals

Species	Country Where Now Found	Number in Wild	Date Count Published	Main Threats
Yangtze River dolphin	China	a few tens	2000	Habitat loss due to pollution; collisions with ships; dam building.
Vancouver Island marmot	Canada	24	2002	Logging; weather changes.
sheath-tailed bat	Seychelles	less than 50	1999	Unknown
Javan rhino	Indonesia and Vietnam	less than 60	2002	Hunting for its horn; habitat loss due to clearing of forest.
northern hairy-nosed wombat	Australia	65	1998	Habitat loss; competition for food with introduced farm animals.
hispid hare	India and Nepal	110	2001	Habitat loss due to farming and human settlement; hunting for food and to protect crops.
dwarf water buffalo	Philippines	between 30 and 200	2002	Hunting; habitat loss due to human settlement, logging and farming; disease caught from farm cattle.
dwarf blue sheep	China	about 200	2000	Hunting; some habitat loss.
Tonkin snub-nosed monkey	Vietnam	about 200	2000	Habitat loss due to farming; hunting for meat and medicine; military activity.
yellow-tailed woolly monkey	Peru	less than 250	2000	Hunting for food; habitat loss due to farming; capture for pet trade.

Glossary

bounty	a reward offered for the capture or killing of an animal
conservationists	people who wish to save natural resources, plants and animals
DNA	found in every living cell, it contains the organism's genetic characteristics
evolve	develop gradually over time
fossils	remains of long-dead animals or plants preserved in rock, ice or peat
habitats	the environments where animals or plants naturally live
poachers	people who trap and kill animals illegally
predator	an animal that hunts and kills prey
prey	an animal that is hunted by another animal
primate	a group of species including humans, apes and monkeys
reservations	areas set aside for a special purpose
species	a group of animals or plants that shares common features
subspecies	a smaller group within a species

primate

INDEX

Page numbers in **bold** refer to photos or illustrations.

American bison 23, 26–29, **26, 28–29**
  breeding in captivity 28
  hunted by people
    26-27, **26**
'Buffalo Bill' Cody 27, **27**
climate change 8, 21, 24
cloning 9
  DNA needed for 9
  thylacine **11**
  woolly mammoth 9
conservation 14–15, **15**, 17, 24, 28
coral reefs 21, **21**
crocodile 13, 16–17
  Cuban **16**
  farms 17, **17**
  products 16, **16**
endangered species 13–21, 24–25, 30
extinct species 5–11
fossils 8, **8**, 10
habitat loss 13, 18–21, 23, 24
hunting 8, 11, 13, 14, 16, 17, 26–27

mammoth 5–9, **6**, **7**, **8–9**, 23
muriqui—*see* woolly spider monkey
orangutan 19, **19**
polar bear 21, **21**
rainforests 18–21, **18**, **20**
rhino 13–15, **14**, **15**
  breeding in captivity 14
  hunted for horns 14
Siberian tiger 23, 24–25, **24**, **25**
Tasmanian tiger—*see* thylacine
thylacine 5, 10–11, **11**, 23
woolly spider monkey 19, **19**
World Conservation Union Red List 17
zoos 5, 11, 14, 17, 24, 25